In Memory of

Virginia Lee

from
Family
and Friends

Chinese Brush Painting

Traditional and Contemporary Techniques
using Ink and Water

Jane Dwight

Bath · New York · Singapore · Hong Kong · Cologne · Delhi · Melbourne

For Glyn, Sally, Mary, Jenny, and Angela with love

First published by Parragon in 2008

Parragon
Queen Street House
4 Queen Street
Bath BA1 1HE, UK

ISBN: 978-1-4075-1774-2

Author: Jane Dwight
Illustrations: Jane Dwight

For Butler and Tanner
Project editor: Julian Flanders
Designer: Carole McDonald
Photography: Carole McDonald

Printed in China

Contents

Introduction

Chinese Brush Painting is a Western term given to the art form known as "Ink Painting" in China. It is an art form in which special Chinese brushes, used with ink and color on the correct paper, are employed to produce elegant images with brush techniques that show the spirit and proper structure of the subject. It is a very ancient art with traditions, styles, and techniques that differ from those in the West.

For over 3,000 years, Chinese painting traditions have been linked with the arts of calligraphy, poetry, and seal engraving, all of which may appear in a finished picture. Other traditions are different, too. For example, there can be several perspectives in a Chinese landscape (high, deep, horizontal, and misty), and a person is never bigger than a mountain. In the West our receding perspective makes objects, or people, in the foreground larger than anything in the distance. Light and shade are not as significant in Chinese painting as they are in the West.

The three main subject areas in Chinese Art are "figure," "landscape," and "bird and flower" painting. All animals and plants are included in the "bird and flower" category.

Chinese Brush Painting can be divided into two distinct styles: fine brush painting (known as *gongbi*) and free brush painting (known as *xieyi*). *Gongbi* work is created with fine lines and many washes on meticulous (nonabsorbent) paper or silk. This style of painting was championed by the *Yuan Ti Hua*, or Academic artists, of the Song Dynasty (960–1279). The Academic artists used sized silk on which to paint beautifully clear and concise pictures using many layers of ink and color. The Emperor Hizong, of the Song Dynasty, belonged to this school and set up his own painting academy in the Royal Palace. His pictures of birds and flowers, people and places have had a great influence on meticulous art through the ages.

Xieyi painting uses spirited, free brushstrokes that convey the vitality and character of the subject. It is usually painted on absorbent paper in black ink. The Wen Ren Hua, or Literati artists, of the Song (960—1279) and Yuan (1279—1368), and later Dynasties were masters of the freehand style. They captured the spirit, or qi, of their subjects with marvelous brushstrokes. Their paintings were more spontaneous, more emotional; they wrote poems on their pictures and often attempted to evoke the politics and philosophies of the day in their work.

Xieyi is also called freestyle painting, and most beginners will start with this style of work as this book does. In order to build up a catalog of brushstrokes, beginners learn how to paint the Four Gentlemen – bamboo, plum blossom, orchid and chrysanthemum. The ancient scholar painters chose these plants because they each possess characteristics that are worthy of respect and close study. It was also during the Song Dynasty that the three main subject areas of Chinese painting were defined.

This edition begins by looking at the unique equipment needed to paint in this particular style, with a little information about the history of that equipment. The following chapters explain how to begin to use the dedicated equipment to paint your first pictures. Building on the strokes learned in the initial pictures, later chapters will give you a range of subjects from which to pick and choose. Pandas and fish, birds and flowers will all be described, with clear step-by-step instructions about how to paint them.

In the final chapters, there will be special effects to try, giving greater scope to the picture-making process, as well as details about how to back your finished pictures and display them. The "gallery" at the end of the book features pictures using more advanced techniques and materials, something to which the developing Chinese brush painter can aspire.

Chapter One

The Four Treasures

Chinese Brush Painting lessons always begin with a discussion about the brushes, ink, and paper required. Because the paper is thin, this style of painting is done on paper laid over a blanket placed flat on a horizontal surface. In ancient times artists worked at a "Scholar's Desk" on which all the equipment for painting was neatly assembled. Indeed, the artist used the time he spent preparing his desk, and laying out the artist's equipment to think about the work he was going to do, to meditate and to get himself into the right state of mind to achieve fine paintings.

The "Four Treasures" were the most important articles a Chinese artist used, and they are still used to this day. They comprise:

The Ink Stick

The Ink Stone

The Paper

The Brush

The Ink Stick

Traditionally made from soot and glue, the ink stick was invented thousands of years ago. Ink used in the Song Dynasty was made from pine soot and glue and could contain crushed gold or pearls. The ink maker was a valued member of the community, and ancient ink sticks fetch very high prices in the antiques world.

Ink making has developed through the centuries, and a wide variety of beautifully shaped and decorated ink sticks are available today.

There are three main types of soot used. Oil soot, pine soot, and charcoal soot (lamp black). The soot is mixed with glue, as well as a preservative and a fragrance, and the thick mixture is pushed into molds. Although they are usually rectangular, the molds can be in any shape from insects to elephants.

Once the stick has dried, it can be decorated with extravagant pictures. Golden dragons, or silver trees, delicate landscapes, and beautiful ladies are often used as decorative motifs.

The ink stick is ground on an ink stone with a little water to create wonderfully fragrant ink. Oil soot produces a very dense, slightly warm, black color. Pine soot is paler, with blue overtones. Freestyle artists, wanting their strokes to blur and run, prize charcoal soot, which has less glue in it.

You can also buy bottled ink, but this is harder to use, because it is difficult to achieve the right consistency.

It is also possible to buy colored ink sticks. These are made with glue and natural pigments and fashioned in exactly the same way as the traditional soot ink stick (see *Colors* on page 15).

▲ A selection of sticks is shown here. The black ones are ink sticks, one beautifully decorated with an ancient style of calligraphy and the others with gilt figures. The colored sticks will provide a wide range of hues when ground and mixed.

Artist's Tip

Ink sticks vary enormously in price. Generally, the more expensive the ink stick, the finer the ink. My advice is to buy a good-quality ink stick, which will give you a good range of tones and a better finish.

The Ink Stone

The Ink Stone is used to grind the ink stick. The stone has to have a smooth surface, which will produce good thick ink fairly quickly when the ink stick is ground on it. There are a few areas in China where wonderful stones can be found, such as in the Anhui and Jiang xi provinces. Some of the most famous and best quality stones were made from the clay found on the banks of the Yellow River. These were called *Cheng Ni* and were made for the exclusive use of the Emperor and courtiers in the Forbidden City. When the ink stone makers died, their secrets died with them, and some time during the Qing Dynasty (1644–1911) the recipe was deemed lost. It was only twenty years ago when experts announced that after hundreds of experiments they were finally able to make the famous *Cheng Ni* again.

Ancient grinding stones often feature exquisite engraving, and some feature the owner's name and the date they were made. These have become collectors' items over the years and can be very valuable.

▲ A dragon swirls across the lid of this decorative rectangular ink stone.

Artist's Tip

If you are going to buy an ink stone, make sure you choose one with a lid. This will keep your ink fresh for the day.

◀ This large, round ink stone is made of purple clay and is very heavy.

The Paper

Paper was invented in China. It has changed over the last two thousand years, of course, but the paper artists use in China is different than that traditionally used in the West. It is thinner and can be bought in rolls of ten sheets or in large continuous sheets. Westerners often mistakenly refer to this paper as "rice paper," but it is actually made from other natural fibers.

Before paper was invented, painting was done on bamboo strips, on wood and on silk. Some of the earliest paintings ever found in China were done on silk. Two were found in tombs in the Hunan Province that date from the 3rd century BC. They depict figures and mystical animals. Swirling dragons and serpents, fish, and figures are all outlined in ink on large silk banners.

Paper is made from a variety of fibers: hemp, bamboo, mulberry bark, and sandalwood are the main sources. The most famous papermaking town in China is called Xuancheng, and Chinese paper is often referred to as Xuan paper. The amount of "size," or glue, added during the papermaking process will alter the absorbent qualities of that paper. Paper that is "unsized" and contains no glue is called *Sheng Xuan*. It is very absorbent and favored by freestyle painters who use it to capture spirited and lively brushstrokes.

Paper that has a little glue in it is called *ban shu* and has a surface on which it is somewhat easier to paint.

Artists painting in the meticulous style, using layers of paint, prefer the fully sized paper, known as *Sheng Xuan*.

Papers can have delightful additions, such as subtle golden dragons and flowers that appear through the paint as it is applied. Gold and silver leaf can also be added and paper comes in many different colors.

Artist's Tip

For beginners, the best paper to use is bamboo paper because it is slightly less absorbent than the white Xuan paper. However, my advice would be to buy some of each, and practice on the Xuan paper once you have mastered the strokes.

▶ Many objects can be made from paper and, therefore, decorated with Chinese brush painting motifs. In this picture there are a few examples: a book, fan, shaped painting boards, and lampshades, all of which lend themselves to decoration.

▼ Rolls of paper, some handmade and others machine made.

The Brush

Most important of the Four Treasures is the brush. Known as the artist's "true friend," brushes have been made in the same way for centuries. Chinese brushes are always made of natural hair. They come in all shapes and sizes, are often given exotic names, and are distinguished from one another by their hair type. The three main categories of hair type are firm hair, soft hair, and those that are a combination of the two.

Firm-haired brushes tend to be brown and are normally made from horsehair, badger, sable, or squirrel. They are often referred to as wolf-hair brushes and are generally easier to use, being springy and resilient. Beginners should buy a good quality "orchid bamboo" (a) or "plum blossom" (b) brush to help with initial strokes.

Soft-haired brushes are usually white and made from goat or sheep hair. Often called sheep-hair brushes, they are a little more difficult to use. Artists favor them for the wide range of marks they can make. These brushes are ideal for painting flowers.

Combination brushes are also very useful. With wolf-hair in the middle and sheep-hair on the outside, they can provide marks that are the best of both types. Look for "blue tip" (c) for general work or "crab claw" (d) for fine work.

The hairs in a Chinese brush are carefully graded before the brush head is glued into a hollow handle, usually made of bamboo. The brush head is lightly starched to protect it during transportation. The starch will soak off in water. Once loaded the brush should form a fine point.

The tiny loop of ribbon, found at the other end of the handle, allows the artist to hang the brush upside down after use, preventing water from collecting around the neck, which might dislodge the glue. Always rinse brushes in cold water as soon as you have finished with them, then hang them up, tip down, to dry.

Different widths of soft sheep-hair brushes are also available for applying a color wash to the front or back of a painting.

▶ A large brush with a bamboo handle and a combination of hair.

▲ The attractive handle of this porcelain brush was reputed to keep the Emperor's hand cool in the summer, while he painted.

◀ An elegant wine box makes a handy brush container.

Artist's Tip

When first buying brushes it is not worth choosing a small one, as any good brush should give a fine line regardless of its size.

Wolf-hair brushes.

Sheep-hair brushes.

Combination hair brushes.

◄ This bone-handled sheep-hair brush is kept in a box when it is dry to protect it.

► Brush paintings often feature washes as a background or to highlight other colors. A variety of wash brushes are of different sizes are useful for tackling large or small washes.

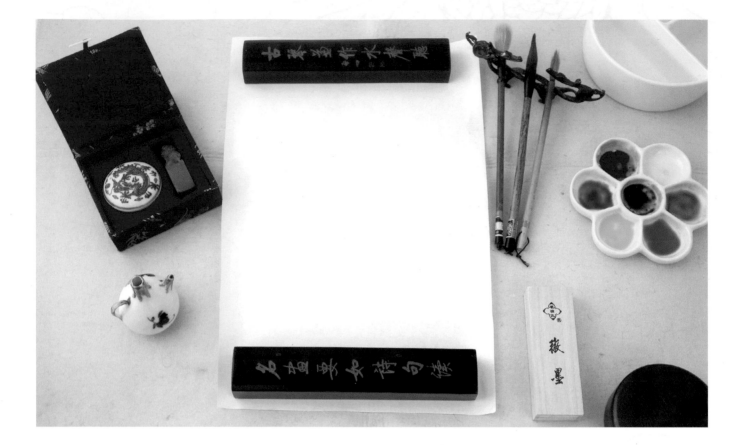

The Scholar's Desk

The Four Treasures will appear in a particular order on the Scholar's Desk. However you will need some additional equipment before you start painting.

Most painting is done with your paper resting on a thick white felt or blanket. This is to prevent the paper from sticking to the surface of the table on which you are working.

You will also need a water container. You can find containers with three sections, which is a very useful way of keeping some clean water available as your painting progresses. But two jars of water, one for rinsing the brush and one for loading the brush, will work just as well.

You will also need one or two weights to help anchor the paper flat for painting, a selection of small white plates, which will be useful for mixing colors and a brush stand to keep wet brushes off the painting surface.

Always be sure to have a roll of paper towels ready in case of spills.

▲ Traditionally, the equipment for the Scholar's Desk is laid out in strict order according to whether the artist is right- or left-handed.

Artist's Tip

Equipment for the Scholar's Desk can be expensive. But the novice can assemble his or her own equipment at no great expense. All you need are two jars for water, a piece of old blanket or sheet on which to rest the paper, and a Chinese brush—an "orchid bamboo" would be ideal. A small bottle of Chinese ink costs very little, or you could use any water-based paints. Old newspapers provide an excellent for practicing new strokes.

Colors

Black ink is the most important medium in Chinese brush painting, and colors are generally only used to augment and enhance the ink strokes. In traditional Chinese art a muted palette is preferred, certainly in landscape painting. A freestyle landscape is usually drawn and textured in shades of ink. Only very light washes of burnt sienna and/or indigo augment the final picture. Brighter colors, such as mineral green and mineral blue, are more often used in meticulous style landscape paintings.

The Chinese palette is made up of organic and mineral colors. The most important mineral colors are mineral green or malachite (*shih lu*), mineral blue or azurite (*shih ching*), and white (*chien fen*). They are often compared to gouache colors because they are opaque. Umber and cinnabar are other mineral colors, although not used as frequently. Organic colors include indigo, carmine, and gamboge yellow, all of which create beautifully transparent washes.

▲ The chrysanthemum dish is useful for keeping the colors separate. A few small flat, white dishes will work equally well.

▼ The basic Chinese palette is muted, but with skillful use of brush and water you can achieve a surprising variety of colors and textures.

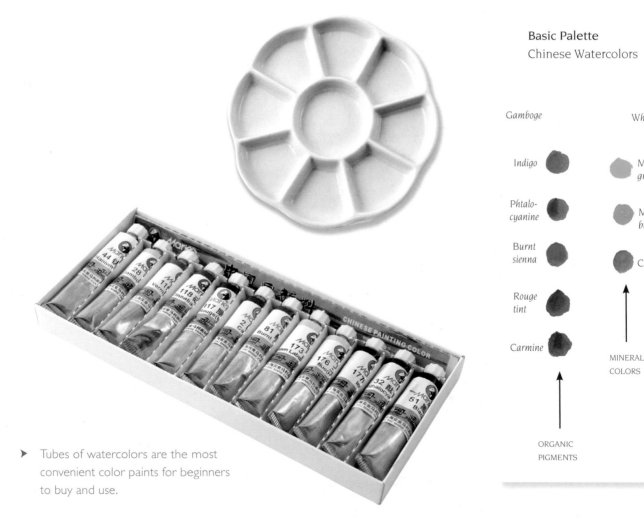

Basic Palette
Chinese Watercolors

Gamboge   *White*

Indigo   *Mineral green*

Phtalo-cyanine   *Mineral blue*

Burnt sienna   *Cinnabar*

Rouge tint

Carmine   MINERAL COLORS

ORGANIC PIGMENTS

▶ Tubes of watercolors are the most convenient color paints for beginners to buy and use.

However, if you are looking to use brighter colors you can select Japanese *Teppachi* colors, although they are not favored by the purists. There are fourteen colors available in the palette, such as blood red, brilliant yellow, and burnt sienna.

The most convenient colors to buy and use are tubes of Chinese watercolors, which you squeeze into a dish and add a little water. However, colors can also be purchased in stick form (see *The Ink Stick* on page 8). These are ground in the same way as the black ink stick, but not on the same ink stone. Use another ink stone for the colors in order to keep the black ink unpolluted.

The very best Chinese colors can be purchased as chips (organic colors) or powders (mineral colors). The organic compounds come in little cardboard boxes. They need to be put in a small dish with a little water to produce the paint. Rattan yellow, obtained from the rattan reed, comes in a block and is poisonous. The powdered mineral colors, such as mineral blue and mineral green, come in tiny envelopes. Pigment glue needs to be added when mixing the powdered paints to keep them from running.

It is helpful to use a chrysanthemum dish for your paints, which enables you to set out your range of colors ready to use.

▲ The best paints come as small chips in boxes or powders in folded envelopes.

▼ This selection of *Teppachi* colors provides a basic palette, which can augment the colors found in a standard box of watercolors.

▲ Beautifully carved in a variety of stones, these seals are large, small, square, rectangular, oval, or irregularly shaped. The little dish of cinnabar paste lies on the left.

Seals

It is traditional to "sign" a finished painting with a seal. The earliest seals—some are two or three thousand years old—were made of clay. Today seals are made from a wide range of materials, such as soapstone, jade, or even gold, though they are normally made of soft stone, which is easier to carve. The seal is rubbed in a container of cinnabar paste and then applied in an appropriate place on the finished picture.

The bottom of each seal has an engraving on it—it may be a piece of calligraphy or a simple image. It might give the artist's name, the village from which he or she comes, a proverb, or an animal. Seals often feature beautiful carving, and for some the making of a seal is an art form in itself.

The seal is added to both sign and enhance the work. Sometimes several seals are used on the same picture, because it is common practice for the artist, the buyer, and a noted art critic to stamp the work. This can increase its value.

Chapter Two

The First Strokes

Before you begin painting, assemble all the equipment you need. This process of setting out the "Scholar's Desk" can be meditative, helping to focus the mind on the task ahead. If you are right-handed, place the brushes, water containers, ink, and color palettes to the right of the blanket. Equipment should go on the left for those who are left-handed.

Choose a comfortable chair that allows you to sit at the table at waist level. Sit upright with your feet flat on the floor, a hip's width apart.

Choosing your paper

Generally speaking, papers from the Far East are much more absorbent than Western watercolor paper. Because of this, strokes that are done slowly will spread and thicken. If you want thinner, crisper lines, then you will need to work quickly. However, as mentioned in Chapter One, bamboo paper is forgiving and, therefore, perfect for beginners.

The three papers pictured below have varying absorbencies. Dry strokes look similar on all of them. Wet strokes will begin to go "fuzzy" at the edges on the semi-absorbent bamboo and absorbant Xuan papers—but not on the fully sized meticulous paper, which contains more glue. Very wet strokes are blurred on the bamboo and Xuan, but the ink "puddles" on the meticulous paper. This shows that the most challenging paper to paint on is the single-ply Xuan.

Semi-absorbent bamboo paper.

Absorbent single-ply Xuan.

Fully sized meticulous paper.

Grinding the ink

1 Put a teaspoon of water into the well of the ink stone.

2 Holding the ink stick upright, grind it in the water with a gentle circular motion. When the ink is thick and sooty enough the ink stick will begin to leave a trail behind it, which is easy to see. To prevent evaporation, always cover your ground ink until it is needed. Dry the end of the ink stick by blotting with a paper towel to keep it from cracking.

Holding and loading the brush

1 Hold the brush gently but firmly, with the index and middle fingers on one side and the thumb on the other. Keep the index and middle fingers apart on the handle of the brush. Keep your shoulders relaxed and hold your elbow off the table.

2 Most painting is done holding the brush upright, with the fingers well above the center on the shaft. However, careful close work will be easier to do if the wrist is resting on the table and the grip on the brush is lower.

3 Before using any brush, make sure it is fully loaded with water. Wipe the excess water out of the brush on the lip of the water container.

4 Dip the brush into the ink and turn it over a couple of times. Try not to "twirl" the brush in the ink, because this will disorganize the hairs at the point. Leave plain water at the neck of the brush.

5 Once again, remove excess ink from the brush by pulling it across the lip of the ink stone. This also helps to straighten the hairs into a point.

The first marks

1 Holding the brush upright, draw a
straight line. Begin on the left with
brief pressure on the tip of the brush
and end with the same brief pressure.
Do several lines and then increase the
pressure on the tip. The resulting lines
will be broader.

    Draw several lines at that pressure
and then increase the pressure again to
paint the widest line possible with your
upright brush. This exercise can be
repeated from right to left on the
paper or from top to bottom and vice
versa. Check, occasionally, that your grip
on the brush has not changed and that
your elbow is still held up. Notice what
the ink does when lines are crossed.

2 Vary the pressure on the tip of the
brush as you paint the next line. Press
and lift, then press and lift again as you
travel across the paper.

3 Keep painting without reloading the
brush to see just how much ink the
brush will hold. Crosshatching like this
will show you how much dark ink runs
into light and vice versa.

4 Try some dots. Hold the brush upright and let the tip make a dot on the paper. Lift the brush off in different directions to see the effect (a). Try twisting the shaft of the brush between your fingers as you paint the dots (b). Change the angle of the brush and, using the whole head, paint a series of very large dots (c).

As you make your initial marks with the brush, try changing the "color" of the ink by changing its density. Dilute jet-black ink with water until you have at least five shades.

Now the varied lines and dots can be repeated in different "colors" (or "states"—see below) of ink.

a

b

c

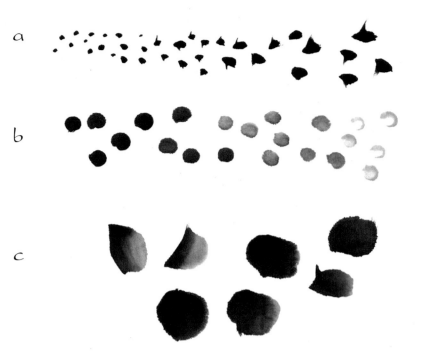

5 There are five basic states of ink, using different tones: "water ink" is made with very pale ink and a lot of water (a); "dry light ink" gives scratchy marks (b); "light ink" is neither very wet nor very dry (c); "dark ink" is the same consistency, with just a change of color (d); and "burnt ink" gives very dry, black marks (e).

Experiment with your mark making, looking out for the contrasts (wet and dry marks, light and dark marks, thick and thin marks).

Pulling the brush over the surface will give a different mark to pushing the brush over the surface.

a

b

c

d

e

a   b   c

Using color

Unlike Western watercolor painting, where the use of black and white is discouraged, the Chinese palette is considerably broadened by the intelligent use of black ink or white paint in a mixture. Sooty ink mixed with yellow, for example, gives a beautiful olive green (a). Ink and carmine red produces a wonderful deep red that is very useful for painting dark peonies or fall leaves (b).

The "indigo" blue made by mixing cyanine blue and ink can be used for painting backgrounds, shadows, and rocks (c). By adding a little burnt sienna to the blue and ink mix, a warmer shadow color appears (d). This can be used on organic subjects, as well as rocks and mountains. Mixing ink with burnt sienna will give a deep brown that is great for animal fur and branches, muddy water, and shadows (e). Green, made by mixing blue and yellow, can be successfully darkened by the addition of ink (f).

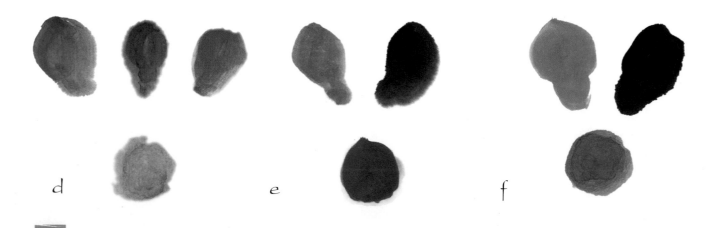

d   e   f

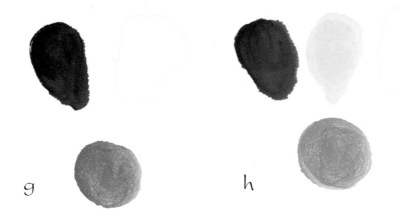

g   h

White should be used with a little more care. It can deaden a picture if over applied. Very pretty, pale pink plum blossoms are painted with a mixture of white and carmine red (g). Adding a little yellow to the mixture will produce a beautiful salmon pink (h). Thin white can be applied to mists and clouds, and thick white spattered lightly over a painting to show falling snow (i). White mixed with blue or with burnt sienna can create the pale colors needed to paint the breast of a bird or the belly of a silvery fish (j). Translucence is achieved with a thin wash of pure organic color, so do not add white to that color beforehand. The mineral colors in the Chinese palette, such as mineral blue or green, are not translucent.

The color swatches on page 24 show the variety of hues that can be produced by adding a little black ink to a color (a–f). Adding white to a color makes the color swatches on this page (g–j).

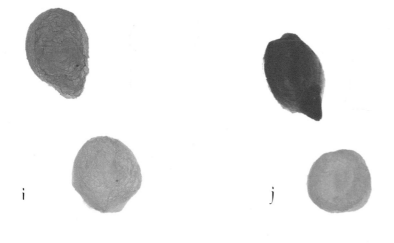

i   j

Loading the brush with color

1 Load your brush with colors in exactly the same way as you did with ink. Make sure the brush is wet first and press out the excess water on the edge of the dish. Now fill three-quarters of the brush with a light color, for example yellow. (Plain water is always left in the last quarter of the brush at the place where the hair joins the handle. This helps with blending and also prevents ink or color from accumulating where the glue holds the brush head into the handle.)

2 Now dip the tip of the brush into blue. Press it a little on the dish to encourage the blue to travel about halfway up the brush. Try painting a few strokes with this yellow and blue mixture to discover what effects can be made. Reload the brush with the same colors and dip the very tip of the brush into red. Pull the brush sideways across the page and you should be able to get a stroke that includes all three colors.

upright brush, tip running centrally

side stroke

lighter pressure on the brush

pressing and flicking strokes

pressing and lifting off the page strokes

three colors

3 Try changing the color in the tip of your brush as you dot paint onto the paper surface (a).

Purple fills the brush with the tip dipped in green. Hold the brush upright and turn it around on the surface of the paper to give a "grape" shape—highlighted with white (b).

Cinnabar and indigo leaves are achieved by filling the brush with cinnabar and then dipping the tip into the indigo. Pressing and lifting the brush as you move it will create a variegated leaf (c).

When trying other color combinations remember to fill the brush with the palest color first. For another attractive stroke, try flattening out the brush tip. Fill the brush with pale green and then dip each side of the wedge into indigo. Pulling the wedge square onto the surface will make a beautiful bamboo stem. By varying the size of the brush and the colors used, a wide variety of stems can be painted (d).

Dry brushstrokes can be made by using the side of the brush that has been filled with two colors (e).

a

b

c

d

press

lift

press

lift

press

lift

press

e

Chapter Three

The Four Gentlemen

The first task of the Chinese Brush Painting student is to learn how to paint the "Four Gentlemen." These are the Plum Blossom, Bamboo, Chrysanthemum, and the Orchid.

Each plant has very different characteristics, and each requires a great deal of practice to paint well. But once mastered they will provide the student with a catalog of strokes with which to paint other subjects.

During the course of their practice, students will also discover how to control the ink flow on the paper, make the ink "colors," and begin to feel more comfortable holding and loading the brush properly.

Plum Blossom

The plum blossom is the national flower of China. It is associated with winter because the plant's delicate flowers arrive at the end of winter, before the new leaves appear. It is a symbol of rejuvenation and, because it seems to withstand the cold, also represents perseverance.

The branches are painted first, and the blossoms are added next. Buds are then painted at the tips of the branches, and dark sepals, stamens, and dots finish the picture. It is a good idea to try a variety of brushes for this exercise.

1 For thicker, larger branches, load a soft-haired brush with medium pale ink. Try not to have the ink too dark or too wet as you press your brush onto the paper. Pull the brush along, pausing briefly to change direction as you go. Branches get thinner toward the tip, so lift the brush into a more vertical position as you move (a). Try this with a wolf-hair brush, too.

Dry ink marks make for an interesting, rougher branch (b). Darker ink should be used for the smaller branches. Apply lighter pressure with the brush to paint the smallest twigs. Because we will be adding plum blossom flowers later, leave the occasional gap in the branch for them (c).

A large branch, painted with wet ink running into dry, and dark twigs and dots, will provide a lovely starting point for adding plum blossoms (d). Contrasts such as these always enhance a picture.

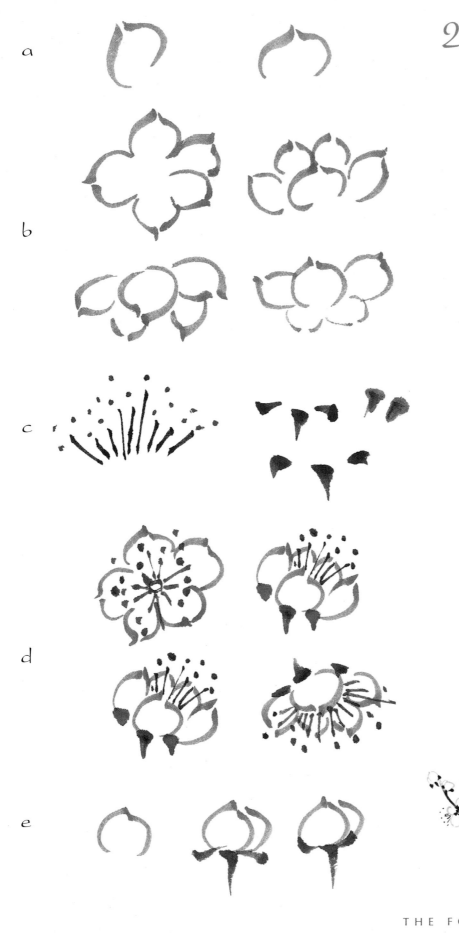

2 The blossoms can be painted using outlines or solid dots. But don't mix the two kinds on the same branch.

For the "outline" method, load a small wolf-hair brush with pale ink. Hold the brush upright and, with the tip of the brush, practice drawing circular shapes in two strokes (a).

Every blossom has five petals, each one of which should be a different size, and none should be perfectly round. Paint a few blossoms in different positions (b).

Once you have painted a selection of blossoms add the stamens and calyx. Often referred to as "tigers' whiskers," the stamens are painted in dark ink with firm, wiry strokes that begin and end with slight pressure. Add tiny pollen dots above the stamens. Beneath the flowers and buds there are dark calyx strokes painted in dark ink, with little nail-like dot strokes (c).

The blossoms themselves will be seen from different angles, with their stamens and calyx in place (d).

Buds, made up of one or two petals, always grow on the tips of the branches (e).

Paint a small branch and add outlined plum blossoms as seen below (f).

f

3 Alternatively, blossoms can be painted using the "dot" method. They are illustrated here in shades of red, but they could be painted in other colors, mineral green or yellow, for example.

Load a small sheep-hair brush with red and paint a small, solid shape, holding the brush upright and twisting it slightly as you press (a). Assemble five dots of differing sizes to make a blossom (b). A row of blossoms, painted at different angles, indicates how to vary the "dot" assembly. Blossoms on the branch will vary in position and tone.

While the flower is still a little damp add the stamens and the calyx strokes (c). These are illustrated in dark red (carmine mixed with ink), but they could be white with yellow pollen if you prefer. Use the tip of a small wolf-hair brush to paint a row of fine "tigers' whiskers" for the stamens, and sprinkle them with round spots of pollen. Use a "nail head" stroke, painted by pressing and flicking the tip of the brush, to give the blossom its calyx underneath the petals. This is usually done with three strokes as illustrated (d).

Buds will just need one or two petal strokes with the calyx below (e).

a

b

c

d

e

4 Paint a branch first and then
arrange the blossoms and buds
on the branch. They should be in
groups at unevenly spaced intervals
and at different angles on the branch,
to make an attractive arrangement.

Bamboo

Symbol of summer, peace, and strength, bamboo is one of the most popular subjects painted in China. It is also one of the most useful plants in the world.

Its hollow canes are used for irrigation channels, cooking vessels, cups, scaffolding, and brush handles, for example, and the leaves of one particular bamboo variety provide the endangered Giant Panda's only source of food.

The bamboo is made up of canes, joints, branches, and leaves, painted in that order.

1 Begin by loading a large brush with pale ink. (The brush can be soft, mixed, or wolf-haired.) Dip the tip into slightly darker ink and, holding the brush upright, press it firmly onto the paper. Twist the brush very slightly and move it quickly upward, stopping and pressing again after a couple of inches. Lift the brush off the stroke in a downward movement. This stroke resembles a calligraphy stroke called the "bone". Paint a row of these strokes, one after another, traveling up to the top of the page. Do not reload your brush. Each cane of bamboo should be painted with one brush load of ink or color (a).

At each joint in the cane paint a darker calligraphy stroke. Use a small wolf-hair brush and dark ink. With the tip of the brush, held upright, begin on the left of the joint. Press a little to the left and downward, then travel back across the gap in a slight arch ending with a flick upward to the left. The middle of the stroke should blend into the cane a little (b).

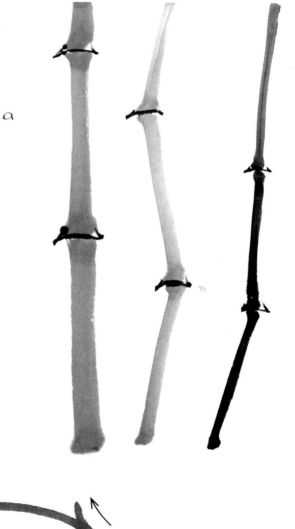

a

b

Paint a few side branches alternately up the canes. Use ink that is darker than the cane but lighter than the joint. With the tip of a small wolf-hair brush draw smaller bone strokes, ending in two or three divisions.

3 Bamboo leaves are painted with a stroke that is almost opposite to the cane stroke. Use any brush with a fine tip loaded with dark ink. Put pressure in the middle of your stroke this time, coming off the paper with the tip of the brush (a). Paint the second stroke smaller than the first and slightly overlapping it (b). This grouping is called a "fish" or "swallow tail." Three leaves in a group become a "goldfish tail" (c). Notice that each leaf is a different size. A "goose landing" describes four leaves in a group (d) and a "swallow flying" five leaves (e).

Paint groups of leaves so that some of them cross over the branch (f).

Paint leaves in groups over the ends of the branches, beginning with the darkest ones. These will be in the front of the picture. Lighter groups of leaves fall behind them, and the most distant leaves will be the palest (g).

a

b

c

d

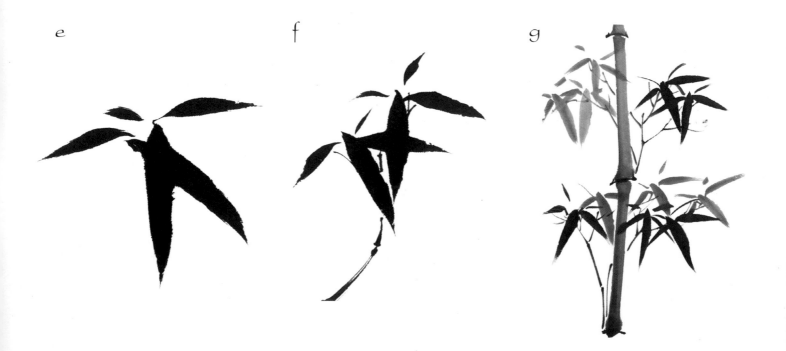

e

f

g

4 In these examples the bamboo plant has been painted in color. Yellow and indigo were mixed in varying strengths to provide a nice contrast. Use more indigo to give a deeper green and more yellow to produce a lighter green. Vary the size of the canes and the colors of the leaves to produce a picture full of attractive contrasts. Try painting bamboo in a variety of reds as well. This is known as lucky bamboo.

Chrysanthemum

Symbol of fall, the bright chrysanthemum will bloom even when it is very cold. Therefore it represents "cheerfulness in the face of adversity," and it is a very popular subject to paint. There are many ways to do it: wild and free with ink and color running together, or carefully and precisely showing each papery petal.

There are two examples of chrysanthemum painting included here, both in the freestyle manner. In the first example, the petals are outlined, and in the second they are painted with a solid stroke. The leaves, stems, and buds remain the same in both examples. Practice the different strokes on newsprint first, before assembling them.

When painting a picture of chrysanthemums, make it easier by beginning with the flowers.

1 To paint the flower center of an open bloom, drop a few dots of dark color onto the paper with a small wolf-hair brush. Using the same brush, paint each petal in two strokes, beginning with a light press at the tip (a). Try to make each petal slightly different. Place the petals around the dots, each stroke coming inward (b).

A bloom painted in side view will need three or four petals pointing upwards, with the rest painted outward and downward (c).

Paint buds with pale gray, inward-curling petals surrounded by a dark ink calyx and stalk (d).

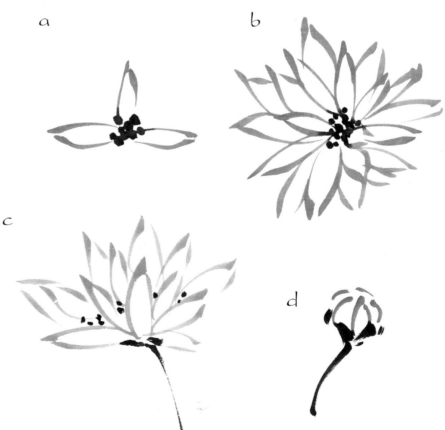

a

b

c

d

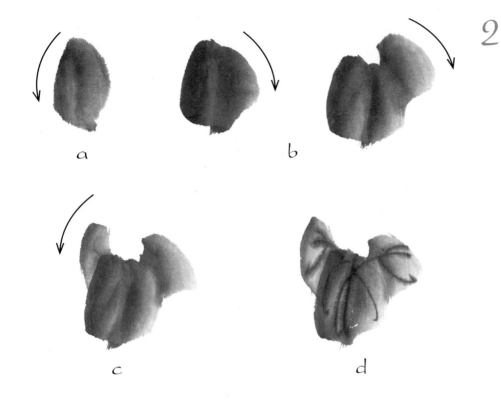

a

b

c

d

2 The chrysanthemum leaves are painted with a large soft-haired or combination hair brush. Load the brush three-quarters full with pale gray ink and press the tip into ink that is a little darker. Using the whole of the brush, make a large, broad dot (a). Add two smaller dots at each side (b). Vary the colors and sizes of these three-dot leaves and paint them all around the chrysanthemum blooms (c). Let them dry a little and then add the veins, using a small wolf-hair brush and darker ink. The veins should blend into the damp leaf (d).

Chrysanthemum stems are sturdy, almost woody, and should be painted with a firm dry ink line, holding the brush upright and weaving among the leaves.

Dark dots, indicating lichens or mosses, enhance the final painting.

Different angles

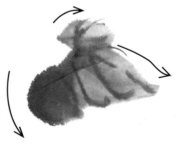

Side view

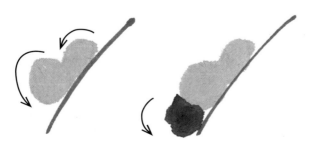
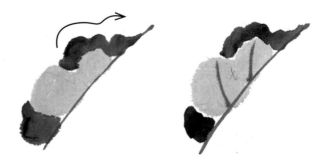

3   The second example, painted in solid strokes, is a more "fancy" variety. Use a small wolf-hair brush for this.

  As before, paint a few dots on the paper for the center of the flower (a). To paint the petals, load the brush with two colors. Fill it with a pale color first, such as lilac, and press the tip into a darker color, such as deep purple.

  With the tip of the brush add little tadpole-shaped strokes around the dots (b). Press the tip of the brush onto the paper and then lift it onto its tip as you make the curly "tail" of the petal. Paint larger petals around the first, and so on, always painting the tail of the stroke toward those initial dots. You will see that the center of the bloom is dark and the outer petals get lighter as you paint (c, d, and e).

a

b

c

d

e

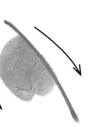

a

b

c

d

4 To finish the picture paint the buds, leaves and branches as before. Try using color this time, instead of ink. The brush could be three-quarters loaded with pale green, for example, with the tip pressed into dark green or orange to give a lovely variety of colors (a and b). Add veins in ink while the leaf is damp (c).

   The firm branch strokes will look good in a darker green or brown. Add a few dots in ink to represent mosses or lichen, for a spectacular finish (d).

Orchid

Delicate and elegant, the tranquil orchid provides the "yin" to the more forceful "yang" of bamboo. The orchid painted here is a simple marsh orchid, and the contrast between the dark, ribbonlike leaves and the pale, fragile flowers makes it an attractive subject. Of all the "Four Gentlemen," the orchid is practiced most by students in China because the strokes used are a valuable skill to master.

Traditionally, the flowers can either be painted as a single bloom on a stem or as several flowers on a spike. If a painting shows several orchid plants, then they should all be of the same variety.

The orchid leaves are long and thin and blow gently in the wind, exposing both the back and front of their surface. Thick and thin strokes capture this movement.

1 Begin by painting the leaves. Use a large wolf-hair brush and dark ink. Begin on one side of the paper, leaving enough room for the leaves to flow. Draw the first leaf with a long arc, pressing and lifting the brush along the length of the stroke, turning the arm and the brush. The movement should come from the shoulder, with the elbow held up (a). The second leaf will begin near the same point as the first and bend either to the left or right, crossing the first leaf at some point. The shape these two leaves make is called the "eye of the phoenix" (b).

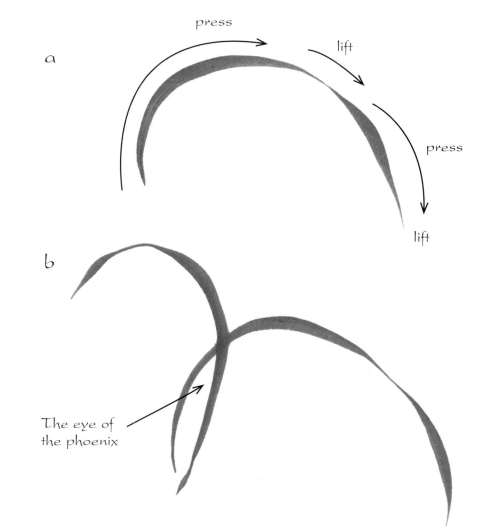

press

lift

a

press

lift

b

The eye of
the phoenix

2 The third stroke should cross the "eye" (c). The fourth and fifth strokes are painted on either side of the original three (d). Notice that each leaf is a different length, and each ends in a different place. More leaves can be added, but this simple five-leaved format should form the basis of the plant.

c

d

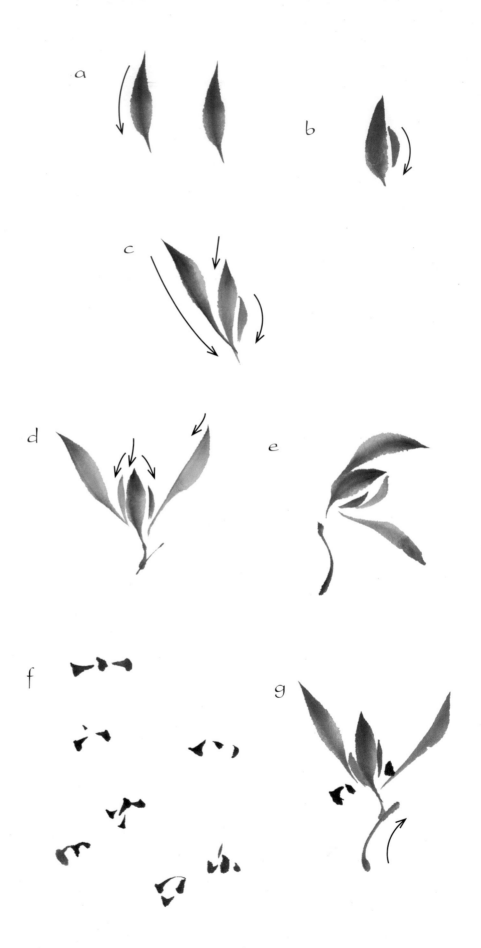

3 The orchid flower has five petals. These should be done in a pale color with a combination hair brush and short strokes. Press lightly in the middle of the stroke, coming off the page on the point of the brush (a). If you are painting several flowers on a spike then imagine they are like your hands, with the fingers acting as the petals. Touch the middle finger to the thumb and move your hands as though they are flowers going up the stem, sometimes nodding to each other, sometimes looking in opposite directions, sometimes upwards, sometimes down. Paint your flowers in the same attitudes so that all the blooms are different but linked.

Start with two strokes, painted close together, for the central petals (b). Next, add a third petal to join the first two (c). The fourth petal should be added on the opposite side, and the fifth one is usually very small and painted anywhere within the flower (d). Vary the positions of the petals and the directions the flowers face (e). It is most important that the petal strokes should all be made from the tip of the petal and move inwards, towards the base of the bloom.

4 Tiny dots painted in darker ink with the sharp tip of the brush are used to finish the flower. Just touch the tip to the paper and lift away quickly leaving a tiny tail (f).

Each flower has two or three darker dots painted around the center, called 'dotting the heart' (g).

With the same brush and slightly paler ink, paint a delicate stem between the flowers, attaching the blooms with tiny side shoots (d, e and g).

5 This finished picture shows leaves, stems, and flowers combined. Just a few delicate blooms lend simplicity to the composition. Try painting an orchid with several more leaves and flowers, remembering not to overdo it and lose the simplicity.

Chapter Four

Broadening Your Repertoire

This chapter includes instructions and advice on how to paint a number of new subjects, experimenting with the strokes learned in the previous chapter. The all-important 'Four Gentlemen' appear again, this time giving you a chance to revise the subjects and begin to include them in more complicated compositions. Fish, flowers, birds and animals are all covered, giving a small taste of this wonderful and very wide-ranging art form.

Fish

Simple fish forms can be painted using a small wolf-hair brush and a little leaflike stroke. These little "minnows" should have eyes, gills, fins, and tails added with the tip of the brush.

1 Painting a larger fish, such as a carp, will require a larger, soft-haired brush. Load the brush with blue and then pick up a little ink on the tip. Paint a large leaflike stroke, running the tip of the brush through the middle of the stroke, pressing in the center (a).

   With the tip of a wolf-hair brush and dark ink, paint in the mouth, eyes, gill, and belly. Before the body of the fish is completely dry, the scales should be added. These are done with the tip of the brush and grid of lines (b).

   Next, add the fins and a tail. The dorsal fin running along the top of the fish is painted with a dark line. The lower fins need a little press in the stroke. Two short leaflike strokes complete the tail (c).

a

b

c

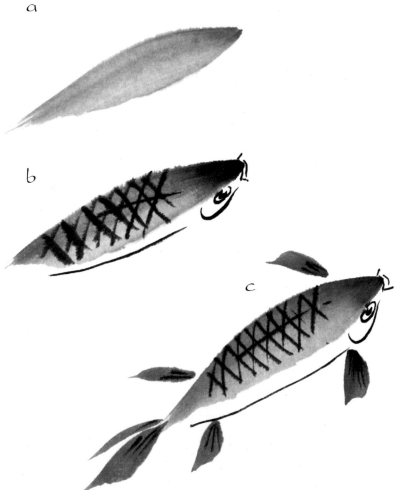

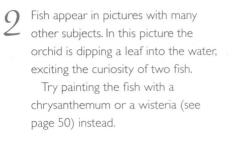

2 Fish appear in pictures with many other subjects. In this picture the orchid is dipping a leaf into the water, exciting the curiosity of two fish.

   Try painting the fish with a chrysanthemum or a wisteria (see page 50) instead.

Wisteria

It is said that each stage of life is represented in the wisteria plant. The fragrant, delicate blooms are childhood, and the whippy tendrils are carefree youth. Sturdy, rough branches support and carry the leaves and flowers, representing maturity.

Begin by painting the flowers. They have four petals, two large and two small. They grow around a central stem, which hangs down from the branches. Mix a pale lilac color, using carmine and sky blue. (Another pretty mauve can be made using carmine and mineral green.)

1 Load a small soft brush with a pale color and paint a medium-sized dot with the brush held at a slight angle (a). Paint a similar dot beside it (b). With a darker tone of purple, add two flat dots for two lower petals (c). To complete the flower, put two spots of yellow in the center (d).

Paint a group of flowers (called a raceme) with small buds at the bottom. Paint a stem running straight through the group, attaching some of the flowers and buds to it (e).

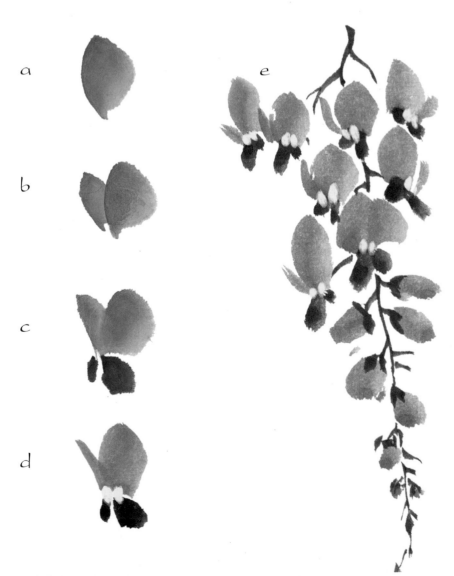

a

b

c

d

e

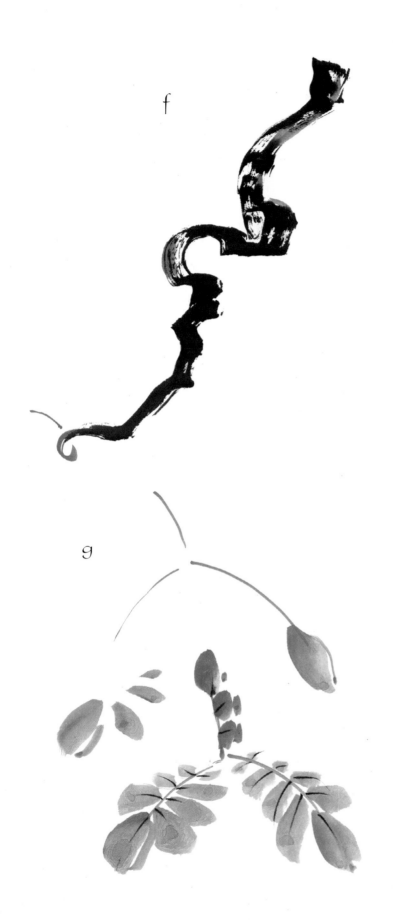

f

g

h

2 The branches should be painted next, either with green or ink. Weave a dry, twisting stroke among the flower groups, and attach each raceme to it (f).

Leaves, in short flat strokes, painted on either side of a central vein, can be a variety of colors: greens, browns, blues and lilacs (g). Add the leaves above the flowers.

Finish the picture with green, swirling tendrils, looping their way through the composition. These should be painted with spirit, using the tip of a springy wolf-hair brush (h).

3 The completed wisteria should hang down from the branch with crowns of leaves cascading above it and tendrils weaving among the foliage. (Try painting several blooms hanging from a branch.) In this picture a branch of bamboo painted in ink completes the scene.

Peony

The beautiful peony symbolizes wealth and distinction and is a very popular decorative motif. It is a large, blowsy flower with many petals and is often likened to a pretty woman, spreading perfume to attract bees and butterflies (or suitors).

1 Begin by painting the flowers. They can be any color although red is the most admired. Fill a large soft brush with deep pink and dip the tip into darker red. Use the whole brush head to draw three petals initially (a). Refill the brush and paint three more petals directly above the first three (b). Continue to add further petals until the flower is large enough (c and d).

a

b

c

d

2 Paint one or two blooms as needed and a simple bud with a few petal strokes (a). Petals can be added to the bud if you want to develop them further.

3 Leaves can be painted with large broad strokes like those used for the leaves of the chrysanthemum. Paint them so that they frame the flower head. Use a large wolf-hair brush and fill it first with pale green. Press the tip of the brush into darker green and, for the occasional leaf, use a little red. Use the side of the brush as you paint the leaf (b). Add veins in ink while the leaf is still damp (c and d).

a

b

c

a group of leaves

d

4 The stem, firm and woody, winds through the leaves. Use the wolf-hair brush to paint the stem in dark green or brown.

5 Once the peony flower is dry, paint a large mineral green dot in its center. Curly stamens, painted with a thick white and yellow mix, should surround the dot.

6 To finish the picture, why not add a butterfly? Butterflies are painted in a similar fashion to the wisteria flowers. Use a small wolf-hair brush, filled with the color of your choice, and paint a large stroke for the upper wing, and a smaller stroke for the lower one. Smaller lines represent the wings on the other side of the body. Wait for the butterfly to dry a little and then add the body. Decorate the wings with dots and lines, perhaps looking at a picture of a butterfly to copy the pattern on its wings.

Birds

Traditionally, Chinese painting is divided into three distinct subject areas: figures, landscapes, and birds and flowers. The category "birds and flowers" also includes animals and all plants.

Birds are very popular subjects, appearing in all sorts of pictures. They often convey hidden meanings. The crane represents longevity and happiness, the owl heralds disaster, and an eagle represents strength.

The simplest way to place any bird in a painting is to draw the head and body as small and large egg shapes initially. Once the direction the bird is facing is established in relation to its body, then that shape can be fleshed out with features and feathers.

In the finished picture on page 58, the two birds are looking in different directions: one shows its back and the other its breast.

1 It helps to paint the beak and the eye of the bird first using the tip of a small wolf-hair brush and ink (a). The top of the head should be added next, in two round strokes, and in the color of your choice. Add some darkness at either side of the eye at this point (b). The throat is usually pale; here, white and gray with a broad dot stroke is used. One large green stroke painted with the side of a wolf-hair brush gives the bird its back (c).

The wing feathers are suggested with small dark strokes on each side of the body, and the tail feathers are painted with a couple of strong dry marks. Notice the little curved line that gives the bird its foot (d).

2 Begin the second bird in the same way as the first, painting the beak and eye first (e).

Paint the top of the head and the back in the same color, using short dot strokes for the back. The pale chest and belly are painted in overlapping dot strokes (f).

Load a small wolf-hair brush with a darker color to paint the wing feathers and tail. Three dark lines, curling around the branch, indicate the bird's feet (g).

3 Here, the birds are sitting in a plum blossom tree, but they could be standing under a peony or sitting among wisteria flowers, playing in the bamboo or chirping among the chrysanthemums. There are endless variations to try.

Pandas

The remarkable panda is a living treasure in China. An endangered species, it lives a solitary life in the forests of Eastern China, feeding on the leaves and shoots of its favorite bamboo species. Great efforts are being made to ensure this lovely animal survives. As long as its habitat remains undisturbed, and the particular bamboo it eats does not die out, then the panda has every chance of survival.

Looking at photos of a panda will help you determine its size, its distinctive markings, and the way it moves. Preliminary sketches will help you to establish the proportions and colors you'll need. This, of course, is true for any subject.

1 To paint a panda, use a large, soft brush filled with dark ink. Notice that the face is almost hexagonal in shape. The ears are painted with a curling stroke at the top of the head, on the corners of the hexagon (a).

If you can imagine a line cutting the hexagon in half, then the eyes and eye patches fall just below that line. Begin a curling stroke with the tip of the brush and then press the brush onto the paper to make each distinctive eye patch (b).

Paint the black nose with a leaflike mark and add the jowls in paler ink. The whole head can be outlined in pale gray broken lines, which give a furry effect (c).

2 Refill the brush with dark ink and paint
a broad sweeping line for each arm,
ending with a dry brushstroke for the
paw and claws (d).
  Repeat this stroke for the legs (e)
and then add pale fur around the
panda's belly.

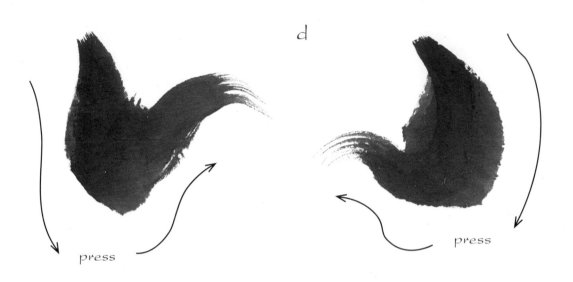

d

press

press

e

Your panda could be painted sitting in a bamboo grove chewing his favorite food.

Chapter Five

Special Effects

So far the emphasis has been on learning how to manipulate the brush and how to paint a series of definite strokes. As with every new art form, getting to know the equipment and its basic use is important. Equally important, however, is the experimental side. This chapter introduces the painter to a series of techniques that will help you achieve a variety of different effects. Some are as simple as painting on a crushed paper surface. While others introduce a number of new materials, such as milk and salt, and encourage you to experiment with new media.

Crushed paper

It is possible to achieve an intense "marbled" effect with Chinese paper in a very simple way. First, a clean sheet of paper should be crushed (crumpled) or "scrunched" by hand. But it is important that the crushing should be limited to a specific area of the paper.

If you want to paint rocks, for example, then the paper should be crushed just where you are going to paint them.

Crush the paper thoroughly, then press it flat again with your hands. Fill a brush with ink, wiping out the excess, and, holding the brush horizontally over the area, scrape the brush over the crushed surface. The ink will leave a pretty, marbled effect. Other colors can be added at any stage and an outline added, if needed.

Orchids or chrysanthemums look good with rocks that have been painted in this way.

If you want to paint trees, then the paper can be crushed in vertical lines, smoothed out, and painted in the same way. This will produce gnarled tree trunks with rough bark.

Try using the crushed paper to paint other features, such as mountains or large lotus leaves.

Water

The use of water works best on absorbent Xuan paper. It is very subtle but can give lovely results, as this picture of a galloping horse illustrates.

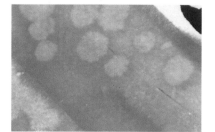 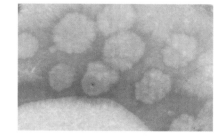

Scatter, or paint, drops of clean water where you want them. Let it soak into the paper but do not let it dry. Lightly paint a single wash of color over the drops of water and then let the picture dry.

This can be an effective way of putting variations onto the surface of leaves, or rain into skies.

Experimenting with the technique is a good way to discover its potential.

White paint

White paint is another useful resister. An object painted in white will show up well on a dark background.

Try painting a bird or a flower in white paint onto white Xuan paper. Then leave it to dry. Turn the paper over and paint a dark wash over the back. You will see that the white image will become more prominent and obvious on the front.

The cockatoo in this picture was painted in this way. Once dry, the image was turned over and a wash of blue painted across the back.

This can be a particularly effective way of painting the moon in the dark evening sky, for example, achieving an almost translucent effect.

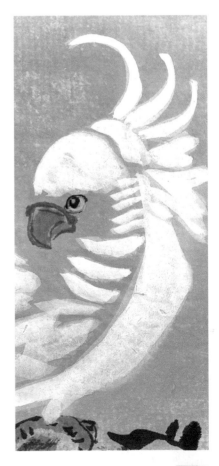

Milk

Use milk to paint a shape on the page. Milk or cream acts as a resister in almost the same way as water. Because milk contains fat it will soak into the paper and dry, resisting any color painted over it. As a result the special effects are much easier to achieve. Milk can be spattered or dripped, painted on in lines or dots, or applied as a solid form for something such as a fish or the moon.

Once the paper is dry, paint a wash over the top, and the milk-shapes will appear.

The spots and stripes on this frog (opposite) were painted with cream and left to dry.

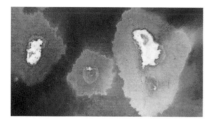

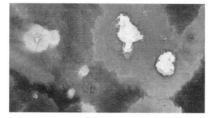

Salt

Adding salt to a wet painted surface is a wonderful way to produce a textured finish, for example, to an animal skin or a landscape background. It can also be used to make leaves look more lively or to give water a rain-splashed surface. Here, it is used to suggest the feathers on a chicken's back.

Paint a large patch of ink or color onto the paper. Sprinkle it with rock salt and let it dry. Remember to blow off any excess salt before you finish the painting.

Cooking salt will give a finer texture, because it produces smaller speckles.

Printing

A printing tool can be made by crumpling or wadding a piece of scrap paper into a ball. Dip the ball into liquid paint and then press it onto a clean sheet of paper. Prints or print marks made this way can be turned into almost any subject with a few deft strokes.

In the picture of the flowers pink print marks were turned into roses by adding a few leaves and curly strokes for petals. The two brown print marks in the example below were turned into storks.

Wet in wet

If you are painting feathers or fur, try painting "wet in wet"—adding a second layer of ink or paint while the first layer is still wet. This is a process with a lot of possibilities and is worth experimenting until you get it right.

1 For the ducks in this picture, start by using pale gray ink strokes.

The eyes and beaks were done with a dry brush tip, on a dry surface, and provide a nice contrast to the rest of the birds.

2 Working quickly while the gray ink was still wet, the artist added several dark lines to represent the feathers. They blurred and smudged on the wet surface, producing the soft marks needed.

Painting cats and squirrels this way will help you achieve the necessary softness of the animals' fur.

Spraying color

Color can be sprayed onto a surface in various ways. A toothbrush loaded with color and then scraped across the bristles with something solid, such as a piece of cardboard or a thumbnail, will spatter color over the surface of a painting. Holding the brush a little closer to the picture and regulating the amount of spray can cover fairly small areas.

Using a spray can or bottle will also produce a nice effect, and a more regular one, too.

This picture of two birds on a branch has been given a spray of green paint with a toothbrush to provide green foliage.

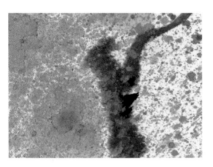

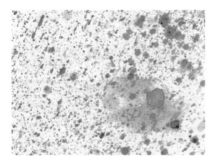

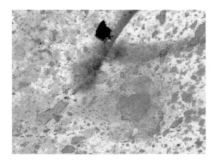

A crane dances across the wetlands surrounded by feathery reeds that have been given a light spray of yellow ocher with a toothbrush.

In these pictures of bamboo at night, the moon was sprayed on with ink from a spray bottle. The bamboo was painted in ink first and then left to dry before a circle cut out of newspaper was placed onto the unfinished painting. Spraying over the top of the newspaper circle, and then removing it, created a perfect full moon.

Chapter Six

Displaying Your Work

Once you have started Chinese Brush Painting, you will quickly build a collection of finished work. Chinese paper is generally very thin, and it's a good idea to buy a portfolio to keep your paintings flat and safe. Work that you want to display will need to be backed to provide a second layer of support. You can then either mount and frame your pictures, or use them to make greetings cards, for example. You can also purchase blank white Chinese paper fans or lamp shades. Once decorated, these make ideal gifts.

Backing

A finished painting needs to be backed for two reasons. Backing gives thin paper the support it needs as well as stretching the painting completely flat so that it will be ready for mounting and framing.

For backing, first gather all the things you will need: ready-to-use wallpaper paste, a wide flat brush, a piece of backing paper that is the same weight or heavier than that of the painting, cut so that it is at least 2 inches bigger all the way around. A board that is larger than the backing paper will also be needed, along with a pencil, a ruler, and a craft knife.

1 Place the painting face down on a clean, flat surface. A board on a table is ideal. Use a wide pasting brush to apply the ready-to-use wallpaper paste onto the middle of the back of the picture. Brush the paste outward with each brushstroke, going toward the edges first (a) and then toward the corners (b). Once the back of the picture is covered with paste, and there are no air bubbles left, wipe away the paste from the table around the picture (c).

2 Roll up the backing paper and, beginning on one side and remembering to leave a 2-inch border, gently unroll it onto the painting, pressing with either the palm of the hand or a mounting brush to adhere (d).

3 Next, apply paste to the outer edge of the border, leaving a dry edge around the picture itself (e).

4 Using both hands, carefully lift the picture (f) and place it face up on the board. (To simplify things, you could have the board propped vertically against a wall.) Press the glued border onto the board to adhere (g). Do not press the picture itself onto the board.

5 Leave the board in a dry place for 24 hours, until it is completely dry. Use the ruler and pencil to draw cutting guidelines around the picture, leaving a small border. Cut out the picture carefully, using the craft knife (h).

Mounting and framing

To mount and frame your finished work in the traditional Western style, you will need to purchase a picture frame that will complement the painting. It should have glass and a back.

1 Choose a complementary color for the bristol board (or mat), and cut it so that it frames the picture (a). Tape the top of the picture to the back of the bristol board. Place another piece of plain paper behind the picture to protect it.

2 Put the mounted picture into the frame and fasten the back into place, complete with a tie in the usual way, and your picture is ready for hanging (b).

You can, of course, have this done at a framing store or simply buy an already-made frame and mat of the appropriate size and color.

Chinese scrolls

In China, artworks in the home are changed several times a year. Very often the pictures will reflect the time of year. This process of changing pictures is made much easier because each picture can be rolled up and tied like a scroll. Although the painting is backed in the way previously described, in China the picture will be finished with beautiful silk borders and a firm paper backing that is often waxed to make it slippery and easy to roll. A wooden rod at the top and bottom of the scroll will allow it to hang well. The whole process of producing scrolls like these is an art form in itself, and it is difficult to find experts in the West.

Oriental decoration

With all the equipment required, Chinese Brush Painting cannot really be described as a flexible art form. However, there are plenty of accessories that you can buy to decorate with your newfound artistic skills. These decorative accessories are great to display around your house but also make beautiful and thoughtful gifts for others.

Included here are a number of ideas, many of which you can do yourself but some of which require you to seek outside help. On the following pages you will find step-by-step instructions to help you produce your own unique homemade greeting cards and directions on how to decorate a Chinese paper fan.

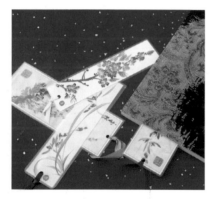

◄ Bookmarks
Bookmarks are a very easy gift to make. You will need to paint a tiny picture using a wolf-hair brush. The picture can be long or square, oval or rectangular. It should then be laminated to make it more long-lasting. Punch a hole at the bottom of the laminated picture and attach a ribbon to finish the bookmark.

▲ Lamp shades
Paper lamp shades give a special glow to a room, and they can be decorated to fit in with any color scheme. White lamp shades have been painted pink and yellow in this picture. The motifs were painted on after the color wash had dried.

◄ Ceramics
If you have the opportunity to attend a ceramics class in your area, then the skills you have learned in this book can be translated into designs that look great on pots and plates, on tiles and cups. The enamel paints might damage your brushes; so wash them carefully with shampoo afterward to preserve them. The results are often worth the hard work and will make delightful ornaments.

◀ ▲ **Mats and coasters**

Successful pictures can be turned
into place mats and coasters that make
superb gifts. It is also possible to get
color photocopies made into place
mats. Some research will be necessary
to find the nearest mat producer, and
it is always worth asking if they can
make other products with your images,
such as tote bags, trays, breadboards,
mouse mats, or coffee cups.

▶ **Gift tags**

Card companies often sell paper
scraps from their cards in the form of
circles or ovals, squares or rectangles.
They will sell a bag of these very
cheaply. Paint a variety of designs on
the scraps, using your new skills. Make
a hole in the bottom of the picture,
using a hole punch, and attach a ribbon
to finish the gift tag.

Make your own greeting cards

A homemade card is always very much appreciated. It shows that someone has spent time creating something especially for you. Painting a small picture right onto folded paper can make the simplest greeting card. But you can be a little more creative.

1 Try cutting out a piece of cardboard (a) and then gluing a square of brightly colored paper onto the cardboard (b). You will need some soft paper for the next step. Any hemp paper will do, and Xuan or grass paper works, too.

2 Paint an image that is smaller than the square of paper and let it dry (c). With a wet brush, make a circle around the painting. Once the paper is wet it will tear more easily, leaving an attractive soft edge around the picture (d).

3 Glue this in the center of the paper square and finish off with a few drops of glitter or other embellishments. Many choices can be found in your local craft or sewing store (e).

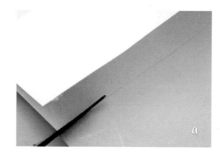

Try this process using the subjects
you have learned. Plum blossom
looks pretty with sparkling pollen;
orchids can be painted with silver
leaves, for example.

Decorated fans

Blank paper fans are easy to find in art stores and Asian emporiums. They make lovely gifts that can be decorative as well as useful. Remember that the fan has two sides to illustrate. Any of the Four Gentlemen will look pretty, but bamboo and plum blossom are a little easier to paint. The long leaves of the orchid make it slightly more difficult to execute over a folded surface. The fans illustrated here (see photos) are intended to be framed and displayed.

1 Fans have always been widely admired in China, so much so that you can buy fans without handles specifically for framing and displaying (a). However, the one we are going to decorate has a handle (b) and can still be used as a fan. You will need to open and flatten the fan as firmly as possible. Press the folds flat, using both hands (c). This surface will be a little uneven to paint on, but with a large brush and bright colors it should be fairly easy.

2 To paint a chrysanthemum like the one illustrated, fill a large wolf-hair brush with pink and orange. Begin with a few dots and add the curling petals until the bloom is large enough (d). Paint a smaller bud to the right of the bloom. Use a variety of colors and shapes to paint the leaves and add the branches (e). Add the leaf veins in a darker color with a finer brush.

3 Once the flower is dry, paint a few more petals in a deeper red to finish the bloom, and add a little wasp or butterfly (f). (For a fuller description of how to paint a chrysanthemum, see page 38.)

Chapter Seven

Gallery

This gallery shows a range of pictures, painted by the author, intended to whet the appetite of those new to Chinese Brush Painting. These paintings have been chosen to inspire you to recreate similar images using the techniques you have learned, while introducing you to new ones to develop. There are pictures painted in the meticulous fine-brush style, called *gongbi*, such as *White Hibiscus*. There are also expressive freestyle pictures, such as *Wisteria*, which features brushstrokes from the *xieyi* tradition. A short description of each picture gives an indication of what type of paper, or silk, the picture was painted on, as well as some brief information on how the painting was actually created.

Red Lotus with Dragonfly

This picture was painted on nonabsorbent meticulous paper. First the dragonfly and lotus were outlined in ink with a fine-line brush. They were then painted with several layers of color using soft brushes. This makes them stand out against the soft background of burnt sienna and indigo.

Pansies

These flowers were painted on absorbent single-ply Xuan paper, using a large sheep-hair brush filled with three colors. This enabled the petals to be executed in one stroke. Ink marks gave the pansies their distinctive faces. The calligraphy below is bold and lively, too, adding to the dynamic atmosphere.

Fruit in a Bowl
(previous page)
Painted on double-ply Xuan paper using a large sheep-hair brush, the fruit has been deliberately "softened" to provide a nice contrast with the simple, clean lines of the bowl. Absorbent paper is ideal for creating this type of effect.

Calligraphy in Batik

Black tissue paper was used for this work. Using an old brush, swirls of diluted bleach were painted lightly across some of the paper. Next, the calligraphy was painted in warm wax onto the middle of the tissue paper (using old brushes that could be thrown away). Diluted bleach was then used to remove the rest of the black color. The wax preserved the calligraphy, which says "fish."

White Hibiscus

A copy from an ancient master, this picture is painted on silk. The outline was painted in ink, then thin layers of paint were applied using two soft brushes (one to apply the color and one to blend it). A further wash of white was painted over the back of the flower.

Grapes

This is an exercise in the art of *bai miao* or "ink and line" painting. These grapes were sketched from real life first before being carefully drawn in ink on meticulous paper. The layers of ink washes, painted over the grapes, grape leaves, and backgrounds, were created by holding two brushes. The painting took several days to complete, because each layer had to be left to dry.

Mountain Farm

The idea for this picture was taken from a larger picture painted by famous artist Qu Lei Lei. It was painted on absorbent Xuan paper using a small wolf-hair brush to create the farmhouse and finer lines. Washes and dots of bright color were applied to give the composition an autumnal air.

Wisteria (page 95)

Painted on single-ply Xuan with a "mountain horse" brush, this is an example of a free-style painting that shows several contrasts: dry and wet strokes, dark and light strokes, and thin and thick marks. Contrasts are important in Chinese painting and lend to the spirit, or *qi*, of the picture.

Glossary of Terms

Bai miao: Traditional ink and brush line drawing

Ban shu: Lightly sized paper

Blue tip: Large combined hair brush

Cheng Ni: Yellow River clay ink stones

Chi or qi: The spirit

Chien fen: White

Chip colors: Organic colors in chip form (sold in small boxes)

Cinnabar paste: Printing paste for use with seals

Crab claw: Combined hair brush for fine line work

Four Gentlemen: Bamboo, orchid, chrysanthemum, and plum blossom plants

Four Treasures: The ink stick, ink stone, paper, and brush

Gongbi: Fine brush work

Meticulous paper: Nonabsorbent paper

Mineral blue: Blue paint made from azurite, often called "stone blue"

Mineral green: Green paint made from malachite, often called "stone green"

Mountain horse: A popular brush made from fairly stiff horse hair

Orchid bamboo: Long-handled wolf-hair brush

Plum blossom: Short-handled wolf-hair brush

Powdered colors: Mineral colors in powder form (sold in envelopes)

Scholar's Desk: The artist's table and equipment

Sheng Xuan: Unsized paper

Shih ching: Azurite, a type of blue mineral

Shih lu: Malachite, a bright green mineral

Shu Xuan: Fully sized paper

Size: A gelatinous solution containing glue used in glazing paper

Teppachi colors: Dishes of color made in Japan

Wash brush: Wider sheep-hair brushes for doing color washes

Wen Ren Hua: Painters of the "Literati School"

Xieyi: Free brushwork

Xuan paper: Absorbent paper, so called because it is made in Xuancheng, Anhui Province, in central China. It is mistakenly called "rice paper" in the West. Green sandlewood is the most common wood used in Xuan papermaking.

Xuancheng: Center of papermaking in China

Yuan Ti Hua: Painters of the "Academic School"

Suppliers and Credits

United States

Dick Blick Art Materials
P.O. Box 1267
Galesburg, Illinois 61402–1267
General info: 1 (800) 933–2542
info@dickblick.com
international: 001 (309) 343–6181
international@dickblick.com
www.dickblick.com

Jerry's Artarama
5325 Departure Drive
Raleigh, North Carolina 27616
1 (800) 827–8478
www.jerrysatarama.com

Australia

Art Requirements
1 Dickson Street
Wooloowin,
Queensland 4030
(0061) 07 3857 2732

Eckersley's Art & Crafts
97 Franklin Street
Melbourne
Victoria 3000
(0061) 03 9663 6799

Hong Kong

Man Luen Choon
International Supplies
2nd Floor, Harvest Building
29–35 Wing Kut Street
Hong Kong
(00852) 2544 6965
art@manluenchoon.com
www.manluenchoon.com

UK

Louisa S.L. Yuen Oriental Arts
5 Gardner Street
Brighton
East Sussex BN1 1UP
01273 819 168

Guanghwa Company
7–9 Newport Place
London WC2H 7JR
020 7437 3737
customers@guanghwa.com
www.guanghwa.com

Ying Hwa Co. Ltd.
14 Gerrard Street
London W1D 5PT
020 7439 8825

A special thank you to Louisa Yuen from Oriental Arts in Brighton, England for the loan of Oriental Painting equipment for the equipment section.

Index